Content

Mawlid of The Pride of Creation

Author's Introduction 3
Transliteration Rules 6
1 – Intention/Niyyah 7
2 - We Begin with Bismillah 9
3 - The Opening Poem 11
4 - Words of Your Creator 15
5 – Qur'an 17
6 - The Mirror of Creation 21
7 - The Greatest of All Trees 23
8 - Why Do We Make Salawat? 27
9 - The Description of Prophet 31
10 - The Story of Mawlid 35
11 - For the Sake of Muhammad | Ya Nabi 39
12 -Welcome Ya Rasulallah / Ṭalaʿa 'L-badru 41
13 - Grant Us Ya Allah / Salla 'Llahu 43
14 - Supplication 45

Additional Nasheeds by Ali Elsayed

Let Us Celebrate Mawlid 53
The Love of Muhammad 55
My Nation 57
How Can I Praise 59
The Sun of Guidance 61

Author's Introduction

أَعُوذُ بِاللهِ مِنَ الشَّيْطَانِ الرَّجِيمِ بِسْمِ اللهِ الرَّحْمٰنِ الرَّحِيمِ
ā‘ūdhu billāhi mina’sh-shayṭāni ’rrajīm
Bismillāhi ’r-Raḥmāni ’r-Raḥīm
I seek the protection of Allāh from the accursed Satan
In the name of God, the Beneficent, the Merciful

"Faith is the fruit of the nourished soul. The soul's nourishment is love for Allah ﷻ and His Prophet ﷺ"

Praise be to Allah ﷻ, lord of the worlds. The Beneficent, the Merciful.

Peace and blessings upon Sayyidna Muhammad ﷺ, his family and his companions.

Further more, all thanks and praise to Allah ﷻ for granting us the success (tawfeeq) to write and compose this Mawlid book, "Mawlid of the Pride of Creation". We gave it this title because it was the favorite title for one of the Great Shaykhs in the Naqshbandi Sufi way, the late Shaykh Abdullah Al-Fa'iz Addagistani (q). He would use it whenever he would speak about Sayyidna Muhammad ﷺ.

Reciting and reading Mawlid is important in the life of Muslims nowadays, because praising the Prophet helps to increase one's appreciation and love for Sayyidna Muhammad ﷺ. After belief in Allah ﷻ, the love a Muslim has for Sayyidna Muhammad ﷺ is the most important factor in his or her spiritual life. If love is missing, one's faith (Iman) is missing as well. The more we have love for our Prophet, the more our Iman will increase.

You can not love what you do not know. In order to love Sayyidna Muhammad ﷺ, a believer must get to know him. That is why we wanted to write this Mawlid in English. Our intention is for the Mawlid gatherings and recitations to become a vehicle for people to learn something about the greatness of Sayyidna Muhammad ﷺ.

Although listening to the Mawlid recited in Arabic brings blessings and mercy upon those attending, for those who do not speak Arabic, they are missing a huge benefit that comes only with understand the meaning of the nasheeds and poems. Understanding leads to love, and love for our Prophet equates faith.

We ask that Allah ﷻ to make our intentions pure, to accept from us these humble deed, and to grant this Mawlid success (tawfeeq), and grant those who recite it the honor of attaining real love for Sayyidna Muhammad ﷺ

The poor servant in need of Allah's mercy,
Ali Elsayed

Transliteration Rules

To simplify reading the Arabic names, places and terms are not transliterated in the main text. Transliteration is provided in the section on the spiritual practices to facilitate correct pronunciation and is based on the following system:

Symbol	Transliteration	Symbol	Transliteration	Long Vowels	
ء	’	ط	ṭ	آ	ā
				ى	
ب	b	ظ	ẓ	و	ū
ت	t	ع	‘	ي	ī
ث	th	غ	gh	**Short**	
ج	j	ف	f	◌َ	a
ح	ḥ	ق	q	◌ُ	u
خ	kh	ك	k	◌ِ	i
د	d	ل	l		
ذ	dh	م	m		
ر	r	ن	n		
ز	z	ه	h		
س	s	و	w		
ش	sh	ي	y		
ص	ṣ	ة	ah; at		
ض	ḍ	ال	al-/’l-		

1 – Intention / Niyyah

أَعُوذُ بِاللهِ مِنَ الشَّيْطَانِ الرَّجِيمِ بِسْمِ اللهِ الرَّحْمٰنِ الرَّحِيمِ

ā'ūdhu billāhi mina'sh-shayṭāni 'r-rajīm
Bismillāhi 'r-Raḥmāni 'r-Raḥīm
I seek the protection of Allah from the accursed Satan
In the name of God, the Beneficent, the Merciful

Oh Allah, our intention for coming here together
is to praise Your Beloved Prophet and Messenger.
By doing so, we intend to obey Your order.
Through doing so, we seek Your nearness and pleasure.

Oh Allah, we are also here because we are lovers, because we love Your Beloved and wish to be with him forever. Oh Allah, we thank you for this magnificent honor.

Oh Allah, grant us the power and ability to leave the delusion of thinking we have power or ability, and to reach the conclusion that only You have power and ability.

Oh Allah, it is You who granted us success to gather here tonight, to wash away our sins with showers of light, and to taste the heavenly fruits of eternal delights.

Oh Allah, we know we can never praise Your Prophet in a befitting manner; or come close to describing what You've bestowed on him of status and favors; for He is Your Beloved, and You are Allah the Lord of Grandeur and Power.

Oh Allah, please accept these humble deeds from us.
Grant us forgiveness and continued success,
to praise Your Beloved until our last breath.

Fatiha

2 – We Begin with Bismillah

اللهُمَّ صَلِّ وَسَلِّمْ وَبَارِكْ عَلَيْهِ وَعلَىْ آلِه ***Allāhuma ṣalli wa sallim wa bārik*** ***'alayhi wa 'alā ālih*** O Allāh raise higher, bless and send peace on him and his family

We begin by acknowledging our helplessness and need,
for we know that all good things from Allah proceed.
His Messenger informed us in a holy hadeeth:
"No benefit will come from any deed,
which does not begin with Bismi 'l-Lāh".

(Bismi 'l-Lāhi 'r-Raḥmāni 'r-Raḥīm) (x3)

We follow by planting in heavens some seeds,
by praising our Lord and taking heed
of the advice in heavens our Prophet received,
from the father of the Prophets of Tawheed,
Sayyidna 'Ibrahim Khalīlullah:

(Subḥana Allah, wa 'lḥamdulillah, wa la 'ilāha 'illa 'l-Lāh, wa 'l-Lahu 'akbar (x3)

Praising the Prophet is part of our creed.
The one who was told in the Quran to read.

Sayyidna Muhammad whom Allah decreed,
that on the day of judgment, he will intercede
for the sinful servants of Allah.

Ṣalātullah salāmullah ala Taha Rasūlillāh
Ṣalātullah salāmullah ala Yasīn Ḥabibillah (x2)

اللهُمَّ صَلِّ وَسَلِّمْ وَبَارِكْ عَلَيْهِ وَعلَىْ آلِه
Allāhuma ṣalli wa sallim wa bārik 'alayhi wa 'alā ālih
O Allāh raise higher, bless and send peace on him and his family

3 - Opening Poem

اللهُمَّ صَلِّ وَسَلِّمْ وَبَارِكْ عَلَيْهِ وَعلَىْ آلِه

Allāhuma ṣalli wa sallim wa bārik
ʿalayhi wa ʿalā ālih

O Allāh raise higher, bless and send peace on him and his family

For as long as the stars will shine
Ya Rabbi ṣalli ʿala Muḥammad
And even after their light declines
Ya Rabbi ṣalli ʿala Muḥammad
When the moon waxes and wanes
Ya Rabbi ṣalli ʿala Muḥammad
For every drop of water and rain
Ya Rabbi ṣalli ʿala Muḥammad
For every ocean, river or spring
Ya Rabbi ṣalli ʿala Muḥammad
For every leaf the trees sustain
Ya Rabbi ṣalli ʿala Muḥammad
For every seed the fruits contain
Ya Rabbi ṣalli ʿala Muḥammad
For every pebble, speck, or grain
Ya Rabbi ṣalli ʿala Muḥammad
From before the time began
Ya Rabbi ṣalli ʿala Muḥammad

until after no time remains
Ya Rabbi ṣalli ʿala Muḥammad
For whatever Your knowledge contains
Ya Rabbi ṣalli ʿala Muḥammad
For everything Your Power sustains
Ya Rabbi ṣalli ʿala Muḥammad
For the order Your wisdom maintains
Ya Rabbi ṣalli ʿala Muḥammad
For as long as Your sovereignty reins
Ya Rabbi ṣalli ʿala Muḥammad
For the Deputy you've ordained
Ya Rabbi ṣalli ʿala Muḥammad
To represent You in Your domains
Ya Rabbi ṣalli ʿala Muḥammad
He is the greatest of all of your signs
Ya Rabbi ṣalli ʿala Muḥammad
He is the master of all mankind
Ya Rabbi salli ala Muhammad
He never said no or complained
Ya Rabbi ṣalli ʿala Muḥammad
The highest honors he attained
Ya Rabbi ṣalli ʿala Muḥammad
You brought him to Qaba Qawsain
Ya Rabbi ṣalli ʿala Muḥammad
Nearer than two bows of length
Ya Rabbi ṣalli ʿala Muḥammad
By form he was not constrained
Ya Rabbi ṣalli ʿala Muḥammad
His light is in everything
Ya Rabbi ṣalli ʿala Muḥammad

From his light you've created all things
Ya Rabbi ṣalli ʿala Muḥammad
The Throne, the tablet, the pen
Ya Rabbi ṣalli ʿala Muḥammad
The earths and the heavens
Ya Rabbi ṣalli ʿala Muḥammad
Humans, angels and Jinn
Ya Rabbi ṣalli ʿala Muḥammad
For the sake of the Prophet's kin
Ya Rabbi ṣalli ʿala Muḥammad
For the mother of Al-Hasanain
Ya Rabbi ṣalli ʿala Muḥammad
For the sake of Sayyidnal-Hasan
Ya Rabbi ṣalli ʿala Muḥammad
For the sake of Sayyidnal-Hussain
Ya Rabbi ṣalli ʿala Muḥammad
For the sake of Thaniya ithnain (Abu Bakr)
Ya Rabbi ṣalli ʿala Muḥammad
For the sake of the one with fair-mind (Umar)
Ya Rabbi ṣalli ʿala Muḥammad
For the sake of Thoon-Noorain (Uthman)
Ya Rabbi ṣalli ʿala Muḥammad
For the sake Allah's Lion (Ali)
Ya Rabbi ṣalli ʿala Muḥammad
For all the Prophets and Saints
Ya Rabbi ṣalli ʿala Muḥammad
For the sake of all Saliheen
Ya Rabbi ṣalli ʿala Muḥammad
May we all be forgiven
Ya Rabbi ṣalli ʿala Muḥammad

May you erase our sins

Ya Rabbi ṣalli ʿala Muḥammad

May you grant us to visit his shrine

Ya Rabbi ṣalli ʿala Muḥammad

May we see him in our dreams

Ya Rabbi ṣalli ʿala Muḥammad

May we meet at the Pond

Ya Rabbi ṣalli ʿala Muḥammad

May we drink from his holy hand

Ya Rabbi ṣalli ʿala Muḥammad

May we join him in heavens

Ya Rabbi ṣalli ʿala Muḥammad

اللهُمَّ صَلِّ وَسَلِّمْ وَبَارِكْ عَلَيْهِ وَعلَىٰ آلِه

Allāhuma ṣalli wa sallim wa bārik
ʿalayhi wa ʿalā ālih

O Allāh raise higher, bless and send peace on him and his family

4 - The Words of Your Creator

مَولايا صلِّ وسَلِّم دَائِماً أبَداً
عَلى حَبيبِك خَيرِ الخَلقِ كُلِّهِمِ

Mawlaya ṣalli wa sallim da'iman 'abadan
'Ala Ḥabeebika khairi 'l-khalqi khullihimi
My lord, send blessing and greetings continuously and eternally upon Your Beloved, the best One in all of creation!

We try to praise you with words
Words only veil your greatness.
What can one say in your praise?
Can glory be described?

Mawlaya ṣalli wa sallim da'iman 'abadan
'Ala Ḥabeebika khairi 'l-khalqi khullihimi

We try to praise you with words
as many before us tried.
Even though their words are better,
they too must have felt ashamed.

Mawlaya ṣalli wa sallim da'iman 'abadan
'Ala Ḥabeebika khairi 'l-khalqi khullihimi

Everything has been said about you,

everything which words could say,
but our love compels us to praise,
Even if with the same words.

Mawlaya ṣalli wa sallim da'iman 'abadan
'Ala Ḥabeebika khairi 'l-khalqi khullihimi

The words which best describe you
are the words of Your Creator.
Every word He said about you,
Struck down all limits on your praise.

اللهُمَّ صَلِّ وَسَلِّمْ وَبَارِكْ عَلَيْهِ وَعلَىٰ آلِه

Allāhuma ṣalli wa sallim wa bārik
'alayhi wa 'alā ālih

O Allāh raise higher, bless and send peace on him and his family

5 - Allah's Praise for His Beloved in the Holy Quran

أَعُوذُ بِاللهِ مِنَ الشَّيْطَانِ الرَّجِيمِ بِسْمِ اللهِ الرَّحْمٰنِ الرَّحِيمِ

ā'ūdhu billāhi mina'sh-shayṭāni 'r-rajīm
Bismillāhi 'r-Raḥmāni 'r-Raḥīm
I seek the protection of Allāh from the accursed Satan
In the name of God, the Beneficent, the Merciful

(1) إِنَّا فَتَحْنَا لَكَ فَتْحاً مُّبِيناً

(1) Innā fataḥnā laka fatḥan mubīnā
Verily We have granted Thee a manifest victory. (48:1)

(2) لِيَغْفِرَ لَكَ اللهُ مَا تَقَدَّمَ مِن ذَنبِكَ وَمَا تَأَخَّرَ

وَيُتِمَّ نِعْمَتَهُ عَلَيْكَ وَيَهْدِيَكَ صِرَاطاً مُّسْتَقِيماً

(2) li-yaghfira laka 'l-Lāhu mā taqaddama min dhanbika wa mā ta'akhkhara wa yutimma ni'matahu 'alayka wa yahdīyaka ṣirāṭan mustaqīma
So that Allāh may grant you forgiveness for your faults of the past and for those in the future; and to perfect His favors upon you; and to guide onto a Straight path; (48:2)

(3) وَيَنصُرَكَ اللَّهُ نَصْراً عَزِيزاً

(3) wa yanṣuraka 'l-Lāhu naṣran 'azīza
And Allāh will support you with a mighty victory. (48:3)

(4) لَقَدْ جَاءكُمْ رَسُولٌ مِّنْ أَنفُسِكُمْ عَزِيزٌ عَلَيْهِ مَا عَنِتُّمْ حَرِيصٌ عَلَيْكُم بِالْمُؤْمِنِينَ رَؤُوفٌ رَّحِيمٌ

(4) laqad jā'akum rasūlun min anfusikum 'azīzun 'alayhi mā 'anittum ḥarīṣun 'alaykum bi 'l-mu'minīna Ra'ūfun Raḥīm
A Messenger from yourselves has come to you: it grieves him that you should perish: ardently anxious is he over you: to the Believers is he most kind and merciful. (9:128)

(5) فَإِن تَوَلَّوْاْ فَقُلْ حَسْبِيَ اللَّهُ لا إِلَـهَ إِلاَّ هُوَ عَلَيْهِ تَوَكَّلْتُ وَهُوَ رَبُّ الْعَرْشِ الْعَظِيمِ

(5) Fa 'in tawallaw fa-qul ḥasbiya 'l-Lāhu lā ilāha 'illa Huwa 'alayhi tawakkaltu wa Huwa Rabbu 'l-'Arshi'l-'Aẓīm
But if those [who are bent on denying the truth] turn away, say: "God is enough for me! There is no deity save Him. In Him have I placed my trust, for He is the Sustainer, in awesome almightiness enthroned." (9:129)

(6) إِنَّ اللهَ وَمَلَائِكَتَهُ يُصَلُّونَ عَلَى النَّبِيِّ يَا أَيُّهَا الَّذِينَ آمَنُوا صَلُّوا عَلَيْهِ وَسَلِّمُوا تَسْلِيمًا.

(6) 'Inna 'l-Lāha wa malā'ikatahu yuṣallūna 'alān-Nabiy yā ayyuha 'l-ladhīna 'āmanū ṣallū 'alayhi wa sallimū taslīmā.

Allāh and His angels send blessings on the Prophet: O ye that believe! Send ye blessings on him, and salute him with all respect. (33:56)

Translation of some additional Quranic verses in praise of Sayyidina Muhammad (pbuh):

- ***Say to them (oh Muhammad): If you love Allah, then follow me, Allah will love you ... (3:31)***
- ***Who obeys the Prophet obeys Allah (4:80)***
- ***You did not throw when you threw, it was Allah who threw ... (8:17)***
- ***Allah and His angels continuously send blessings upon the Prophet ... (33:56)***
- ***Verily, We have sent you as a witness, a giver of glad tidings and a warner; so that you (mankind) may assist him, venerate and honor him, and glorify Your lord morning and evening (48:8-9)***
- ***... Surely you are always before Our Eyes (52:48)***

- ***And you are of a tremendous character (68:4)***
- ***And We will continue to give you until you are pleased ... (93:5)***
- ***And We have given you the (river of) Abundance (108:1)***

اللهُمَّ صَلِّ وَسَلِّمْ وَبَارِكْ عَلَيْهِ وَعَلَىٰ آلِهِ

Allāhuma ṣalli wa sallim wa bārik 'alayhi wa 'alā ālih

O Allāh raise higher, bless and send peace on him and his family

6 – The Mirror of Creation

أَشْهَدُ أَنْ لا إِلَهَ إِلاَّ اللهُ وأَشْهَدُ أَنَّ مُحَمَّداً رَسُولُ الله

Ash-hadu 'an lā 'ilāha illa l-Lāh
wa 'ash-hadu 'anna Muḥammadan Rasūlullāh
I bear witness that there is no god but Allah, and I bear witness that Muḥammad is the Messenger of Allah.

Praise be to the only One who has true existence
For their existence, on Him all depends.
He has no partner He has no equal
He is the Mighty Lord, the absolute Sovereign.

He is pre-eternal, He is everlasting.
He needs nothing, He needs no one.
Nothing resembles Him, nothing can contain Him.
He is beyond space; He is beyond time.

Ash-hadu 'an lā 'ilāha 'illa l-Lāh
wa 'ash-hadu 'anna Muḥammadan Rasūlullāh
(x2)

His power is such that it has no limits
He is Mighty, He is Omnipotent
If He says Be to something, it will Be
His power is such, you can't imagine
He sees all and He hears all

He knows all, He is Omniscient
He speaks, He conveys His Messages
He is the living One, He is life giving

As-hhadu 'an lā 'ilāha 'illa l-Lāh
wa 'ash-hadu 'anna Muḥammadan Rasūlullāh
(x2)

Praise be to Him, He created the light of Muhammad
from His light, what magnificence!
For 70 thousand years, He dressed His Beloved.
For 70 thousand years, He gazed upon Him.

He made Muhammad the mirror of creation,
all creation with Prophet begins.
He is the Prophet of Allah from before time,
He will remain so after time ends.

Ashhadu 'an lā 'ilāha 'illa l-Lāh
wa 'ash-hadu 'anna Muḥammadan Rasūlullāh
(2x)

اللهُمَّ صَلِّ وَسَلِّمْ وَبَارِكْ عَلَيْهِ وَعلَىٰ آلِهِ

Allāhuma ṣalli wa sallim wa bārik
'alayhi wa 'alā ālih
O Allāh raise higher, bless and send peace on him and his family

7 - The Greatest of All Trees

اللهُمَّ صَلِّ وَسَلِّمْ وَبَارِكْ عَلَيْهِ وَعلَىٰ آلِه ***Allāhuma ṣalli wa sallim wa bārik*** ***'alayhi wa 'alā ālih*** O Allāh raise higher, bless and send peace on him and his family

عَنْ أَبِي عَمَّارٍ شَدَّادٍ، أَنَّهُ سَمِعَ وَاثِلَةَ بْنَ الْأَسْقَعِ، يَقُولُ: سَمِعْتُ رَسُولَ اللهِّ (ص) يَقُولُ: " إِنَّ اللهَّ اصْطَفَى كِنَانَةَ مِنْ وَلَدِ إِسْمَاعِيلَ، وَاصْطَفَى قُرَيْشًا مِنْ كِنَانَةَ، وَاصْطَفَى مِنْ قُرَيْشٍ بَنِي هَاشِمٍ، وَاصْطَفَانِي مِنْ بَنِي هَاشِمٍ " - مسلم والترمذي

Narrated by Ammar bin Shaddad that he heard Wathilah ibn al-Asqa say, that Sayyidna Muhammad (pbuh) said:
***"Indeed Allah chose Kinanah over other tribes from the children of Isma'il; He chose Quraish over other tribes of Kinanah; He chose Banu Hashim over the other families of the Quraish; and He chose me from Banu Hashim."*— Muslim and Tirmidhi.**

This is a song about a tree,
The greatest of all trees.
Its fruits are men, very special men
with whom Allah is pleased.

In their loins they carried a light,
a very special light.
This light was sent to guide mankind
From darkness into light.

Learning the names of these great men,
our Prophet's forefathers,
is a good way to show respect
to the one who is most honored.

The Names of Sayyidna Muhammad's forefathers up to Sayyidna Adnan:

Sayyidna Muhammad	سَيِّدنا مُحَمَّد
Son of Abdulllah	ابنِ عَبدِ الله
Son of Abdul-Muttalib	ابنِ عَبدِ المُطَّلِب
Son of Hashim	ابن هاشِم
Son of Abdi Manaf	ابن عَبدِ مَناف
Son of Qusayy	ابنِ قُصيٍّ
Son of Kilab	ابنِ كِلاب

Son of Murrah	ابنِ مُرَّة
Son of Ka'ab	ابنِ كَعب
Son of Lu'ai	ابن لُؤي
Son of Ghalib	ابنِ غاَلِب
Son of Fihr	ابنِ فِهر
Son of Malik	ابنِ ماَلِك
Son of An-Nadr	ابن النَّضْر
Son of Kinanah	ابن كِنانَة
Son of Khuzaimah	ابنِ خُزَيمَة
Son of Mudrikah	ابن مُدرِكة
Son of Ilyas	ابنِ إليَاس
Son of Mudhar	ابنِ مُضَر
Son of Nizar	ابنِ نِزار
Son of Ma'ad	ابنِ مَعَدّ
Son of Adnan	ابنِ عَدنان

May Allah be pleased with them,
for carrying the light,

of the Mercy to the Worlds,
the full moon shining bright!

اللهُمَّ صَلِّ وَسَلِّمْ وَبَارِكْ عَلَيْهِ وَعلَىٰ آلِه

Allāhuma ṣalli wa sallim wa bārik 'alayhi wa 'alā ālih

O Allāh raise higher, bless and send peace on him and his family

8 - Why Do We Make Salawat?

اللهُمَّ صَلِّ وَسَلِّمْ وَبَارِكْ عَلَيْهِ وَعلَىٰ آلِه

Allahumma ṣalli ʿala Muḥammadin
wa ʿala 'ālihi wa sallim

O Allāh raise higher, bless and send peace on him and his family

Why do we make salawat on Muhammad?
We will try to answer here,
and the answers are very important,
for everyone to know and share.

First of all, he is Allah's Beloved
Allah's love for him is clear.
And when you praise Allah's Beloved,
to Allah you will become dear.

Allahumma ṣalli ʿala Muḥammad
wa ʿala 'ālihi wa sallim (x2)

Second of all, Allah in His glory,
on Muhammad He sends salawat,
And all the angels everywhere and every time,
they have to praise the Holy Prophet.

Third of all, its Allah's order
It is written in the Holy Quran:
"Oh believers make salawat on Muhammad,
And send him your Salams"

Allahumma ṣalli ʿala Muḥammad
wa ʿala 'ālihi wa sallim (x2)

Fourth of all, when you're making salawat,
it is like taking a shower of light.
It will wash away your darkness,
and will make you shine so bright.

5th of all, when you make salawat,
your prayers will be answered,
for Allah honors your prayers,
when you honor His Beloved.

Allahumma ṣalli ʿala Muḥammad
wa ʿala 'ālihi wa sallim (x2)

6th of all, when you're making salawat,
the angels will be happy with you.
They will send salawat on your behalf,
and ask forgiveness too.

7th of all when you are making salawat,
all beings will join you too.
They will make salawat on Muhammad,

and gift the rewards to you.

Allahumma ṣalli ʿala Muḥammad
wa ʿala 'ālihi wa sallim (x2)

8th of all when you make salawat,
You'll be walking on the road to paradise.
So keep making salawat on Muhammad,
until you see heaven with your eyes.

9th of all, Prophet Muhammad
promised those who make salawat,
that he will intercede for them
In the presence of Allah.

Allahumma ṣalli ʿala Muḥammad
wa ʿala ālihi wa sallim.

10th of all, when we make salawat
with Salam upon the Prophet,
He will know that you've just greeted him
and he will then greet you back.

The gifts of salawat are too many,
that is why we will only count to ten.
But there are a few more we all should know,
you and I and everyone.

For one salawat on Muhammad,
Allah will give you ten.
For ten salawat on Muhammad,
A hundred He will send.

For 100 salawat on Muhammad,
A thousand Allah will give.
For a 1000 salawat on Muhammad
In Eternal Heavens you will live.

Allahumma ṣalli ʿala Muḥammad
wa ʿala 'ālihi wa sallim (x2)

اللهُمَّ صَلِّ وَسَلِّمْ وَبَارِكْ عَلَيْهِ وَعلَىٰ آلِه

Allāhuma ṣalli wa sallim wa bārik
'alayhi wa 'alā ālih

O Allāh raise higher, bless and send peace on him and his family

9 - The Description of Prophet (pbuh) According to Sayyidna Ali (r)

بَلَغَ ٱلْعُلَى بِكَمَالِهِ كَشَفَ ٱلدُّجَى بِجَمَالِهِ
حَسُنَتْ جَمِيعُ خِصَالِهِ صَلُّوا عَلَيهِ وَآلِهِ
اللهُمَّ صَلِّ عَلَى مُحَمَّدٍ وَعَلَى آلِهِ وَسَلَّم

Balaghal ʿulā bikamālihi, kashafad-duja bijamālihi
Ḥasunat jamīʿu khisalihi, ṣallu ʿalaihi wa ʿālihi
Allahumma ṣalli ʿala Muḥammadin wa ʿala ʿālihi wa sallim
(x2)

He reached the highest perfection, he removed the darkness with his beauty.
All his attributes were excellent, send praise upon him and upon his family.
Oh Allah send Your blessings and greetings upon Muhammad and his family.

This is the description of Prophet.
According to the one whom he loved,
according to sayyidna Ali,
the believer's guardian and wali.
The one whose eyes, since he was a child
were filled with the eternal delights,
from gazing upon Muhammad

Balaghal ʿulā bikamālihi, kashafad-duja bijamālihi
Ḥasunat jamīʿu khisalihi, ṣallu ʿalaihi wa ʻālihi
Allahumma ṣalli ʿala Muḥammadin wa ʿala ʻālihi wa sallim (x2).

He was neither tall nor short.
He was right in the middle between both.
His hair was not straight nor curly,
but in between and wavy.
His head was neither large nor small.
His face was round and light brown.
This is the description of Prophet.

Balaghal ʿulā bikamālihi, kashafad-duja bijamālihi
Ḥasunat jamīʿu khisalihi, ṣallu ʿalaihi wa ʻālihi
Allahumma ṣalli ʿala Muḥammadin wa ʿala ʻālihi wa sallim (x2).

His eyes were large and black.
His eyelashes were long and thick.
His bones were large with broad shoulders.
His body hair was well placed and in order,
with a thin line of hair from chest to belly.
His hands and feet were thick and strong.
This is the description of Prophet.

Balaghal ʿulā bikamālihi, kashafad-duja bijamālihi
Ḥasunat jamīʿu khisalihi, ṣallu ʿalaihi wa ʻālihi
Allahumma ṣalli ʿala Muḥammadin wa ʿala ʻālihi wa sallim (x2).

When he walked he walked briskly,
as if walking down an incline.
When he turned to look at a person,
with his full body he would turn.
Between his shoulders rested the seal,
and he is the seal of Prophets.
This is the description of Prophet.

Balaghal ʿulā bikamālihi, kashafad-duja bijamālihi
Ḥasunat jamīʿu khisalihi, ṣallu ʿalaihi wa ʻālihi
Allahumma ṣalli ʿala Muḥammadin wa ʿala ʻālihi wa sallim (x2).

He had the most generous hands.
His heart with no limits expands.
He was the most truthful of people,
and the softest amongst them in nature.
He was the noblest of his kind through his blood line.
The noblest in all of creation
This is the description of Prophet.

Balaghal ʿulā bikamālihi, kashafad-duja bijamālihi
Ḥasunat jamīʿu khisalihi, ṣallu ʿalaihi wa ʻālihi
Allahumma ṣalli ʿala Muḥammadin wa ʿala ʻālihi wa sallim (x2).

When they saw him, at first they feared him.
Once they got to know him they loved him.
Those who tried to describe him
would often say about him;
"We have not seen, and we have yet to see
Anyone who resembles he"
This is the description of Prophet.

Balaghal ʿula bikamalihi, kashafad-duja bijamalihi
Ḥasunat jameeʿu khisalihi, sallu ʿalaihi wa ālihi
Allahumma salli ala Muhammadin wa ʿala ālihi wa sallim (x2)

اللهُمَّ صَلِّ وَسَلِّمْ وَبَارِكْ عَلَيْهِ وَعَلَىٰ آلِهِ

Allāhuma ṣalli wa sallim wa bārik
ʿalayhi wa ʿalā ālih
O Allāh raise higher, bless and send peace on him and his family

10 - The Story of His Birth

اللهُمَّ صَلِّ وَسَلِّمْ وَبَارِكْ عَلَيْهِ وَعلَىْ آلِه

Allāhuma ṣalli wa sallim wa bārik
ʿalayhi wa ʿalā ʾālih

O Allāh raise higher, bless and send peace on him and his family

Please listen carefully and be present.
We are about to present,
the story of the great present
Allah gave to His creation.

Ṣalla 'Llahu ʿalaih (x3)
Wa ʿala 'ālihi

This is the story of the birth
of the Master of heavens and earth.
A gem no one can know it's worth,
except the Lord of creation.

Ṣalla 'Llahu ʿalaih (x3)
Wa ʿala 'ālihi

When it was time to send the soul
of the Master of all the worlds,
Gibreel was sent to inform all

the servants in creation.

Ṣalla 'Llahu ʿalaih **(x3)**
Wa ʿala 'ālihi

Oh Gibreel, go and tell the worlds
about this most blessed birth.
This light which I have sent to earth
was created before creation.

Ṣalla 'Llahu ʿalaih (x3)
Wa ʿala 'ālihi

Amina has received this light,
which will turn darkness into light.
In her vision she saw a light,
which filled up all of creation.

Ṣalla 'Llahu ʿalaih **(x3)**
Wa ʿala 'ālihi

The throne was shaking with delight,
and all the stars were shining bright,
ready to gaze upon the light
of the pride of all of creation.

Ṣalla 'Llahu ʿalaih (x3)
Wa ʿala 'ālihi

Everything glorified Allah

with Subhana Allah, and Alhamdulillah,
Allahu akbar and La ilaha illa Allah.
It was the dhikr of all of creation.

Ṣalla 'L-lahu ʿalaih (x3)
Wa ʿala 'ālihi

On the night of the blessed birth,
representatives from other worlds
came to witness here on earth,
the Mercy to all of creation.

Ṣalla 'Llahu ʿalaih (x3)
Wa ʿala 'ālihi

Angels, Asiya and Mary
came to witness the glory
of the greatest event in the history
of events in all of creation.

Ṣalla 'Llahu ʿalaih (x3)
Wa ʿala 'ālihi

When it was time for his birth,
Amina saw heavenly birds,
and three banners covering the earth
announcing the pride of Creation.

Ṣalla 'Llahu ʿalaih (x3)
Wa ʿala 'ālihi

Soon after she gave birth,
The full moon was born on earth,
prostrating with his index finger raised
thanking the Lord of creation.

Ṣalla 'Llahu 'alaih (x3)
Wa 'ala 'ālihi

(This is the place where We Stand Up in veneration of the Beloved of Allah (pbuh)!

صَلَّى اللهُ عَلَى مُحَمَّدْ صَلَّى اللهُ عَلَيهِ وَسَلَّمْ

Ṣall-Allāhu 'alā Muḥammad
Ṣall-Allāhu 'alayhi wa sallam x(2)

11 - Ya Nabi Salam ʿAlaika

> يَا نَبِيْ سَلامْ عَلَيكَ   يَا رَسُولْ سَلامْ عَلَيكَ
> يَا حَبِيبْ سَلامْ عَلَيكَ   صَلَوَاتُ الله عَلَيكَ
>
> **Yā Nabī salām ʿalayka   Yā Rasūl salām ʿalayka**
> **Yā Ḥabīb salām ʿalayka   Ṣalawātu 'l-Lāh ʿalayka**
> *Greetings upon you oh Prophet, greetings upon you oh Messenger*
> *Greetings upon you oh Beloved, Allah's Salawat is upon you*

The whole world was shining so bright,
shimmering with praise and delight.
The perfect One was born on such a night,
the full moon Mawlay Muhammad.

Yā Nabī salām ʿalayka   Yā Rasūl salām ʿalayka
Yā Ḥabīb salām ʿalayka   Ṣalawātu 'l-Lāh ʿalayka

Mercy to all of the worlds,
read the book and you'll find these words.
Rejoice then for the most blessed birth
of Mawlay Sidi Muhammad.

Yā Nabī salām ʿalayka   Yā Rasūl salām ʿalayka

Yā Ḥabīb salām ʿalayka Ṣalawātu ʾl-Lāh ʿalayka

Be happy Muhammad's nation,
your Prophet owns the highest station.
You became the greatest nation
for the sake of Mawlay Muhammad.

Yā Nabī salām ʿalayka Yā Rasūl salām ʿalayka
Yā Ḥabīb salām ʿalayka Ṣalawātu ʾl-Lāh ʿalayka

For his sake Allah forgives all sins,
all nations one day will run to him.
The sinners will enter heavens
for the sake of Mawlay Muhammad

Yā Nabī salām ʿalayka Yā Rasūl salām ʿalayka
Yā Ḥabīb salām ʿalayka Ṣalawātu ʾl-Lāh ʿalayka

12 - Welcome *Ya Rasulallah* / Ṭala'a 'l-Badru 'Alayna

Ṭala'a 'l-badru 'alayna , welcome ya Rasūlallāh
Wajabash-shukru 'alayna, thank You thank You ya
'Allāh

Oh what a grant oh what a favor
Allah has gifted this nation
By sending us His Beloved
Upon him endless salutations

Ṭala'a 'l-badru 'alayna , welcome ya Rasūlallāh
Wajabash-shukru 'alayna, thank You thank You ya
'Allāh

Rejoice then with Allah's mercy
And rejoice with Allah's favor
If you follow prophet Muhammad,
you should know that you have been favored

Ṭala'a 'l-badru 'alayna , welcome ya Rasūlallāh
Wajabash-shukru 'alayna, thank You thank You ya
'Allāh

When we honor you, we gain honor

When we praise you, our faces shine
When we love you, Allah loves us
You are the greatest sign amongst His signs

Ṭala'a 'l-badru 'alayna, welcome ya Rasūlallāh
Wajabash-shukru 'alayna, thank You thank You ya 'Allāh

Oh Allah upon him send Your mercy
And upon him also send Your blessings
And grant us his intercession
On the day when only he is addressing (You)

Ṭala'a 'l-badru 'alayna, welcome ya Rasūlallāh
Wajabash-shukru 'alayna, thank You thank You ya 'Allāh

13 – Grant Us / Ṣalla 'l-Lahu ʿala Muḥammad ﷺ

Ṣalla 'l-Lahu ʿala Muḥammad
Ṣalla 'l-Lahu ʿalayhi wa sallam

Oh Allah grant us a good ending – **Ya 'Allāh ya 'Allāh**
Accept from us what we are sending **Ya 'Allāh ya 'Allāh**
Grant us gifts from your treasures – **Ya 'Allāh ya 'Allāh**
Your treasures are never ending – **Ya 'Allāh ya 'Allāh**

Ṣalla 'l-Lahu ʿala Muḥammad
Ṣalla 'l-Lahu ʿalayhi wa sallam

Grant our souls the great station – **Ya 'Allāh ya 'Allāh**
Of meeting the pride of creation – **Ya 'Allāh ya 'Allāh**
send upon him endless blessings – **Ya 'Allāh ya 'Allāh**
Endless love and salutations – **Ya 'Allāh ya 'Allāh**

Ṣalla 'l-Lahu ʿala Muḥammad
Ṣalla 'l-Lahu ʿalayhi wa sallam

Grant us to honor Your Beloved
Fill our hearts with his sweet love
Grant us to see him in this world,
and in all the worlds above, all the worlds above

Ṣalla 'Llahu 'ala Muḥammadan
Ṣalla 'Llahu 'alayhi wa sallam

Grant us to meet him at his pond
Grant us to drink from his holy hand
Grant us to join him in heavens
Grant us and Your grants are so grand **(x4)**

Salla 'Llahu 'ala Muhammad
Salla 'Llahu 'alayhi wa sallam

14 – The Final Supplication
(from Mawlid Ad-Daiba'i Book)

اللهُمَّ صَلِّ وَسَلِّمْ وَبَارِكْ عَلَيْهِ وَعَلَىٰ آلِه

***Allāhuma ṣalli wa sallim wa bārik
'alayhi wa 'alā ālih***

O Allāh raise higher, bless and send peace on him and his family

(1) الحَمْدُ لله رَبِّ العَالَمِينَ. اللهُمَّ صَلِّ وَسَلِّمْ وَبَارِكْ عَلَيْهِ وَعَلَىٰ آلِه وَصَحْبِهِ أَجْمَعِينْ. جَعَلَنَا اللهُ وَإِيَّاكُمْ مِمَّنْ يَستَوجِبُ شَفَاعَتَهُ، وَيَرجُوْ مِنَ اللهِ رَحْمَتَهُ وَرَأفَتَه

Alḥamdulillāhi Rabbi 'l-'ālamīn. Allāhuma ṣalli wa sallim wa bārik 'alayhi wa 'alā ālih wa ṣaḥbihi ajma'īn. Ja'alana 'l-Lāhu mimman yastawjibū shafa'atahū wa yarjū mina 'l-Lāhī raḥmatahu wa rāfatah

All praise and thanks belong to Allāh, Lord of all the Worlds. O Lord, bestow Your blessings and grant peace upon our Leader Muḥammad ﷺ his family and all his companions. O Lord, make us and all present amongst those who receive his intercession, and we hope for Allāh's mercy and favor.

(2) اللَّهُمَّ بِحُرمَةِ هَذَا النَبِيِّ الكَرِيمْ، وَآلِهِ وَأَصحَابِهِ التَابِعِينَ عَلَى مَنْهَجِهُ القَوِيمْ، اجعَلنَا مِنْ خِيَارِ أُمَّتِهْ، وَّاسْتُرنَا بِذَيلِ حُرمَتهْ، وَاحشُرنَا غَداً فِي زُمرَتهْ، وَاستَعمِلْ أَلسِنَتَنَا فِي مَدحِهِ وَنُصرَتهِ، وَأَحيِنَا مُتَمَسِّكِينَ بِسُنَّتِهْ وَطَاعَتهْ، وَأَمِتنَا اللَّهُمَّ عَلَى حُبِّهِ وَجَمَاعَتهْ

Allāhumma bi-ḥurmati hadha 'n-nabī il-karīm wa ālihi wa asḥābihi at-tābiʿīn ʿalā minhājihi 'l-qawīm, ijʿalnā min khiyarī ūmmatih, w 'as-turnā bidhayli ḥurmatih, w 'aḥshurnā ghadan fī zumratih, w 'astʿamil alsinatanā fī madḥihi wa nuṣratih, wa aḥyīna mutammasikīna bi sunnatih wa ṭaʿatih wa amitnā 'llāhumma ʿalā ḥubbihi wa jamāʿatih

O Allāh, with the honor of this great leader, his family and companions who took the right path, make us the best of his Community (on the Day of Gathering), cover us with his sanctity. Gather us tomorrow in his group. Use our tongue in praising and defending him. Make us to live holding firmly to his Path (sunnah) and obey him, and make us die loving him and his Community.

(3) اللَّهُمَّ ادخِلنَا مَعهُ الجَنَّةْ فَإِنَّهُ أَوَّلُ مَنْ يَدخُلُهَا، وَأَنْزِلنَا مَعَهُ فِيْ قُصُورِهَا فإِنَّهُ أَوَّلُ مَنْ يَنزِلُهَا، وَأَرْحَمنَا يومَ يَشفَعُ لِلخَلاَئِقِ فَتَرحَمُهَا

Allahumma adkhilna maʿahu 'l-jannata fa-innahu āwwal man yadkhuluhā, wa anzilnā maʿahu fī

quṣūrihā fa innahu āwwal man yanziluhā, w 'ar-ḥamnā yawma yashfa'u li 'l-khalā-iqi fa-tarḥamuhā
O Lord, please cause us to enter the Garden with him, for indeed, he is the first to enter it, and cause us to enter its castles together with him for verily he is the first to enter them. Have compassion on us on the day he intercedes for all creation, for You have mercy upon all of them,

(4) اللَّهُمَّ ارزُقنَا زِيَارَتَهُ فِي كُلِّ سَنَةْ، وَلاَ تَجعَلنَا مِنَ الغَافِلِينَ عَنكَ وَلا عَنهُ قَدْرَ سِنَة

Allāhumma 'rzuqnā zīyaratahu fī kulli sannah, wa lā taj'alnā mina 'l-ghāfilīna 'anka wa lā 'anhu qadra sinah
O Lord, please give us the opportunity to visit him every year. Do not make us amongst those who are negligent in remembering You and remembering him even for a little while.

(5) اللَّهُمَّ لا تَجعَل فِي مَجلِسِنَا هَذَا أحَدًا إلاَّ غَسَلتَ بِمَاءِ التَوبَةِ ذُنُوبَهْ، وَسَتَرتَ بِرِدَاءِ المَغفِرَةِ عُيوبَهْ

Allāhumma lā taj'al fī majlisinā hadhā āḥadan illā ghasalta bi-mā'ī 't-tawbati dhunūbah, wa satarta bi riḍā'i 'l-maghfirati 'uyūbah
O Lord, please render anyone in this assembly who has a single misdeed, cleansed with the water of repentance; and conceal his sins with the garment of forgiveness.

(6) اللَّهُمَّ إِنَّهُ كَانَ مَعَنَا فِي السَّنَةِ المَاضِيَةِ إخوَانٌ مَنَعَهُمْ القَضَاءُ عَنِ الوُصُولِ إِلَى مِثلِهَا، فَلا تَحْرِمهُمْ ثَوَابَ هَذِهِ اللَّيلَةِ وَفَضلَهَا *(رَحِمَهُمْ الله)*

Allāhumma innahu kāna ma'anā fī 's-sannati 'l-māḍīyyati ikhwānun man'ahum al-qaḍā'ū 'ani 'l-wuṣūli ila mithlihā, fa lā taḥrimhum ajra hadhihi 'l-laylati wa faḍlahā (raḥimahumul-Lāh)
O Lord, last year there were friends amongst us who returned to You (Have mercy on them) and thus were unable to be present this year because of Your Decree, so please do not prevent them from partaking of the blessings and rewards of this moment and its importance. (**May Allah have mercy on their souls)**

(7) اللَّهُمَّ اِرحَمنَا إذَا صِرنَا مِنْ أَصحَابِ القُبُورْ وَوَفِّقْنَا لعَمَلٍ صَالِحٍ يَبقَى سَنَاهُ عَلَى مَمَرِّ الدُهُور

Allāhumma 'r-ḥamna idhā ṣirnā min asḥābi 'l-qubūr, wa 'rzuqnā 'amalan ṣaliḥan yabqā sanāhu 'alā mammarri 'd-duhūr
O Lord, have compassion upon us when we become the companions of the grave, and provide us with the earnest attempt to do good deeds that will remain shining throughout time,

(8) اللَّهُمَّ اجْعَلْنَا لِأَلَائِكَ ذَاكِرِينْ، وَلِنَعْمَائِكَ شَاكِرِينْ، وَلِيَوْمِ لِقَائِكَ مِنَ الذَّاكِرِينْ، أَحْيِنَا بِطَاعَتِكَ مَشْغُولِينْ، وَإِذَا تَوَفَّيْتَنَا فَتَوَفَّنَا غَيْرَ مَفْتُونِينْ وَلَا مَخْذُولِينْ، وَاخْتِمْ لَنَا مِنْكَ بِخَيْرٍ أَجْمَعِينْ

*(اللَّهُمَّ اكْفِنَا شَرَّ الظَّالِمِينْ – 3 مرات)

Allahuma ij'alna li-ālā-ika dhākirīn, wa lin'amā'ika shākirīn, wa li-yawmi liqā'ika mina 'dh-dhākirīn, wa aḥyīnā biṭā'atika mashghūlīn, wa idhā tawafaytanā fa-tawafanā ghayr maftūnīna wa lā makhdhūlīn, wakhtim lanā minka bi-khayrin ajma'īn (Allāhumma 'kfina sharra 'ẓ-ẓālimīn- 3 times)

O Lord, please make us amongst those who appreciate and remember what You conferred upon us, and be thankful for Your favors, and recall the Day of Meeting with You. Make us live and be preoccupied with obedience to You. When You cause us to die, let it be without falling into temptation nor let us be forsaken. We beg You, conclude all our affairs with the best of endings. **(Our Lord, ward from us the evil of oppressors, 3x)**

(9) وَاجْعَلْنَا مِنْ فِتْنَةِ هَذِهِ الدُّنْيَا سَالِمِينْ

W 'aj'alnā min fitnatu hadhihi 'l-dunyā sālimīn
Keep us safe from the temptations of this worldly life.

(10) اللَّهُمَّ اجعَلْ هَذَا النَّبِيَّ الكَرِيمَ لَنَا شَفِيعًا، وَارزُقنَا بِهِ يَومَ القِيَامَةِ مَقَامًا رَفِيعًا

Allahumma 'j'al hadhā 'n-nabīi 'l-karīma lanā shafī'an, wa 'rzuqnā bihi yawma 'l-qīyāmati maqāman rafī'a

O Lord, makes this Noble Messenger our intercessor, and - because of his intercession bestow upon us a lofty position on the Day of Judgment.

(11) اللَّهُمَّ اسْقِنَا مِنْ حَوضِ نَبِيِّكَ مُحَمَّدٍ صَلَّى اللهُ عَلَيهِ وَسَلَّمَ شَربَةً هَنِيئَةً مَرِيئَةً لاَ نَظمَأُ بَعدَهَا أَبَدًا، وَاحشُرنَا تَحتَ لِوَائِهِ غَدًا

Allahumma 'sqinā min ḥawḍi nabīyyika Muḥammadin ṣallalahu 'alayhī wa sallam sharbatan hanīyyatan marīyyatan lā naẓmā'ū ba'adahā abadan, wa 'ḥshurnā taḥta liwā'ihī ghadan

O Lord, let us quench our thirst from the Pond of our Prophet Muḥammad ﷺ with an easy and unhurried drink that will cause us to thirst nevermore and gather us under his Banner tomorrow.

(12) اللَّهُمَّ اغفِرْ لَنَا بِهِ وَلأَبَائِنَا وَلأُمَّهَاتِنَا، وَلِمَشَايِخِنَا وَذَوِي الحُقُوقِ عَلَينَا، وَلِمَنْ أَجرَىٰ هَذَا الخَيرَ فِي هَذِهِ اللَّيلَةِ، وَلِجَمِيعِ

الْمُؤمِنِينَ وَالْمُؤمِنَاتْ، وَالْمُسلِمِينَ وَالْمُسلِمَاتْ، الأَحيَاءِ مِنهُمْ وَالأَموَاتْ

Allāhumma 'ghfir lanā bihi wa li-abā'inā wa li-'ummahātinā, wa li-mashayikhinā wa dhawi 'l-ḥuqūqi 'alayna, wa li-man ajra hadhā 'l-khayr fī hadhihi 'l-laylah, wa li-jami'i 'l-muminīna wa 'l-muminār, wa 'l-muslimīna wa 'l-muslimāt, al-'aḥyā'ī minhum wa 'l-amwāt

O Lord, for the sake of his high esteem with You, forgive us, our fathers, our mothers, our teachers, and those to whom we are obliged, as well as those who organized this honored assembly on this night, all believers men and women and all Muslims, men and women, the living as well as those who have passed on.

(13) إِنَّكَ قَرِيبٌ مُجِيبُ الدَّعَوَاتْ *(وَقَاضِيَ الْحَاجَاتْ- 3 مرات)* وَغَافِرِ الذُّنُوبِ وَالْخَطِيئَاتْ *(يَا أَرحَمَ الرَّاحِمِينْ- 3 مرات)*

'Innaka qarībun mujību 'd-da'awāt (wa qāḍiya 'l-ḥājāt- 3 times)
Wa ghāfiru 'dh-dhunūbi wa 'l-khaṭī-āṭ (yā arḥama 'r-rāḥimīn – 3 times)

Verily You are The Near, Answerer of all prayers, (and granting all needs), and forgiving all sins and misdeeds, **(O Most Merciful of the Merciful.)**

(14) وَصَلَّى اللهُ عَلَى سَيِّدِنَا مُحَمَّدٍ وَعَلى آلِهِ وَصَحبِهِ وَسَلَّمْ،

سُبْحَانَ رَبِّكَ رَبِّ العِزَّةِ عَمَّا يَصِفُونْ وَسَلامٌ عَلَى المُرسَلِينَ

وَالحَمدُ لله رَبِّ العَالَمِينْ

Wa ṣallallahu 'alā sayidinā Muhammadin wa 'alā ālihī wa ṣaḥbihī wa sallam. Subḥāna rabbika rabbi 'l-'izzati 'amma yaṣifūn, wa sallāmun 'alā 'l-mursalīn wa 'lḥamdulillāhi rabbi 'l-'āalamīn

May Allāh's blessings be upon Muḥammad ﷺ his family and companions and grant them peace. Glory to thy Lord, the Lord of Honour and Power! (He is free) from what they ascribe (to Him)! And peace be upon the Messengers, and Praise be to the Lord of the worlds. Āmīn.

(الفاتحة)

Al-Fātiḥa

Additional Nasheeds *by Ali Elsayed*

Let Us Celebrate

Let us celebrate let us celebrate - Allah
the birthday of Muhammad, let us celebrate - Allah
Let us celebrate, let us celebrate - Allah
Mawlid 'n-Nabi, ṣalla 'l-Lāhu ʿalaih

The birthday of Muhammad is the birthday of Islam
the only one in creation who can receive Quran
join the celebration and praise him if you can (x2)
Ṣallu ʿala 'n-Nabi ya 'ahla 'l-imān (Oh people of belief)

Let us celebrate, let us celebrate - Allah
the birthday of Muhammad, let us celebrate - Allah
Let us celebrate, let us celebrate - Allah
Mawlid 'n-Nabi, ṣalla 'l-Lāhu ʿalaih

Those who love Muhammad, they always celebrate
They don't need a special month or a special date
They celebrate on Monday and on Tuesday,
They celebrate on Wednesday and on Thursday,
On Friday and Saturday and also on Sunday!

Let us celebrate let us celebrate - Allah
the birthday of Muhammad, let us celebrate - Allah
Let us celebrate, let us celebrate - Allah
Mawlid 'n-Nabi, ṣalla 'l-Lāhu ʿalaih

Mentioning Muhammad makes us very happy
Everyday for lovers is Mawlidu 'n-Nabi
You claim to love the Prophet, oh poor Wahhabis (x2)
But when we celebrate, you are so unhappy

Let us celebrate let us celebrate - Allah
the birthday of Muhammad, let us celebrate - Allah
Let us celebrate, let us celebrate - Allah
Mawlid 'n-Nabi, ṣalla 'l-Lāhu ʿalaih

Let us join the angels, and use every second
They celebrate Muhammad on earth and in heavens
Follow their example and don't be a lemon (x2)
Salli ʿalan-Nabi and be in the presence.

Let us celebrate let us celebrate - Allah
the birthday of Muhammad, let us celebrate - Allah
Let us celebrate, let us celebrate - Allah
Mawlid 'n-Nabi, ṣalla 'l-Lāhu ʿalaih

The Ummah of Islam loves Muhammad
Since Sayyidna Hassan, they praise the Prophet
Up until some Bedouin who came from Najid, (x2)
there was not one Muslim who did not celebrate.

Let us celebrate let us celebrate - Allah
the birthday of Muhammad, let us celebrate - Allah
Let us celebrate, let us celebrate - Allah
Mawlid 'n-Nabi, ṣalla 'l-Lāhu ʿalaih

The Love of Muhammad ﷺ

The love of Muḥammad ﷺ and his family
Is my true religion, my reason to be
And if when I die my sins are too many
The love of Muḥammad ﷺ will rescue me (x2)

Allāhumma ṣalli ʿalā ʾl-Muṣṭafā (x2)
Ḥabībnā Muḥammad ﷺ ʿalayhi ʾs-salām (x2)

May God bless the Bedouin for the question he asked
Which unveiled the secret of the power of love
The answer to which made Abu Bakr whirl
You'll be with the ones whom you love (x2)

Allāhumma ṣalli ʿalā ʾl-Muṣṭafā (x2)
Ḥabībnā Muḥammad ﷺ ʿalayhi ʾs-salām (x2)

For Allāh to love you, obey his command
which says if you love me, then follow Muḥammad ﷺ
to follow Muḥammad ﷺ you must love Muḥammad ﷺ
For how can you follow that which you don't love? (x2)

Allāhumma ṣalli ʿalā ʾl-Muṣṭafā (x2)
Ḥabībnā Muḥammad ﷺ ʿalayhi ʾs-salām (x2)

If you love Muḥammad ﷺ you must love everyone
For his light is truly inside everyone

He's the mercy sent to every one
Only through love can we become one (x2)

Allāhumma ṣalli ʿalā 'l-Muṣṭafā (x2)
Ḥabībnā Muḥammad ﷺ ʿalayhi 's-salām (x2)

My Nation

My nation, my nation,
his tears soaked the ground.
He asked while prostrating
for hours on end.
My nation, my nation
My lord, forgive them.
Grant them salvation
and a happy end (x2)

Allāhumma ṣalli ʿalā Muḥammad
Allāhumma ṣalli ʿalāyhi wa sallim

His nation, his nation
is everyone
in this creation,
and in others as well.
His nation, his nation
are you and me,
All those before us
and those who will be (x2)

Allāhumma ṣalli ʿalā Muḥammad
Allāhumma ṣalli ʿalāyhi wa sallim

My nation, my nation,
at his blessed birth.
He made a prostration

and uttered those words.
My nation, my nation
at his blessed death.
My nation he whispered
with his last breath (x2)

How Can I Praise?

How can I praise the one on whom Allah bestowed
the crown of Honor and Majesty?
The one who was granted by His Lord,
the station of Praise and Glory.

Allāhumā ṣalli wa sallim 'alā
sayyidinā wa mawlanā Muḥammadin
'Adad ma fī 'ilmillāhi ṣalātan
dā'imatan bi-dawāmi mulki 'l-Lāhi

The one for whose sake Allāh created,
all that exists in this creation.
The one who is the master of the worlds,
the owner of the highest station.

Allāhumā ṣalli wa sallim 'alā
sayyidinā wa mawlanā Muḥammadin
'Adad ma fī 'ilmillāhi ṣalātan
dā'imatan bi-dawāmi mulki 'l-Lāhi

No mind can understand your greatness.
No words can describe your beauty.
Imagination can not imagine,
the secrets hidden in your reality

Allāhumā ṣalli wa sallim 'alā
sayyidinā wa mawlanā Muḥammadin
'Adad ma fī 'ilmillāhi ṣalātan

dā'imatan bi-dawāmi mulki 'l-Lāhi

We come to you with nothing to offer,
except this love and this repentance,
for not praising you as we should,
So please grant us your acceptance.

Allāhumā ṣalli wa sallim 'alā
sayyidinā wa mawlanā Muḥammadin
'Adad ma fī 'ilmillāhi ṣalātan
dā'imatan bi-dawāmi mulki 'l-Lāhi

The Sun of Guidance

The sun of guidance has risen
with the birth of Muhammad,
and creation was given
the secret of existence (x2)

'Allāhumma ṣalli wa sallim 'alā nūri 'l-hudā
'Allāhumma ṣalli wa sallim 'alā badri 'd-dujā (x2)

He was created from His light,
from the light of the Almighty.
And this light was dressed with more light,
Since pre-eternity.

'Allāhumma ṣalli wa sallim 'alā nūri 'l-hudā
'Allāhumma ṣalli wa sallim 'alā badri 'd-dujā (x2)

From his light, all things were created,
the tablet and the pen,
the angels and the heavens,
the earth, humans, and Jinn

'Allāhumma ṣalli wa sallim 'alā nūri 'l-hudā
'Allāhumma ṣalli wa sallim 'alā badri 'd-dujā (x2)

If you think you know Muhammad,
please think again.

The only one who knows Muhammad,
Is the One who created him.

'Allāhumma ṣalli wa sallim 'alā nūri 'l-hudā
'Allāhumma ṣalli wa sallim 'alā badri 'd-dujā (x2)

When I saw his light

When I saw his light,
I had to cover my eyes,
in fear for my sight
from his amazing beauty.
No words can describe
the beauty of his light.
In fear for my sight,
I had to cover my eyes (x2)

Ṣalātullah salāmullah ala Taha Rasūlillāh
Ṣalātullah salāmullah ala Yasīn
Ḥabibillah (x2)

A spirit made of light
in the form of the moon.
As if the brilliant stars
were woven into his form.
The limits of my mind
could not contain his light.
In fear for my sight,
I had to cover my eyes (x2)

Ṣalātullah salāmullah ala Taha Rasūlillāh
Ṣalātullah salāmullah ala Yasīn
Ḥabibillah (x2)

Oh Magnificent soul,
What kind of beauty You possess?
for the creator of all

to call you His Beloved?
For 70 thousand years,
He gazed upon your light.
Oh magnificent light,
in Fear for my sight
I had to cover my eyes.

Ṣalātullah salāmullah ala Taha Rasūlillāh
Ṣalātullah salāmullah ala Yasīn
Ḥabibillah (x2)

Muhammad ﷺ Lives - Ṣalla Allah

Ṣalla 'l-Lah 'alā Muḥammad,
Ṣalla 'l-Lah 'alāyhi wa sallam
Ṣalla 'l-Lah 'alā Muḥammad,
Ṣalla 'l-Lah 'alāyhi wa sallam

Allah Almighty, He chose Muhammad
Al-Mustapha, He is Muhammad
Allah Almighty, He loves Muhammad
Habibullah, he is Muhammad

Ṣalla 'l-Lah 'alā Muḥammad,
Ṣalla 'l-Lah 'alāyhi wa sallam
Ṣalla 'l-Lah 'alā Muḥammad,
Ṣalla 'l-Lah 'alāyhi wa sallam

Allah almighty, honored Muhammad
We are His servants, honor Muhammad
Allah Almighty, He loves Muhammad
We are His servants, we must love Muhammad

Ṣalla 'l-Lah 'alā Muḥammad,
Ṣalla 'l-Lah 'alāyhi wa sallam
Ṣalla 'l-Lah 'alā Muḥammad,
Ṣalla 'l-Lah 'alāyhi wa sallam

Muhammad lives, even in his grave
Muhammad lives, Nabi Muhammad
Muhammad gives, even in his death
more than he gave during his life

Ṣalla 'l-Lah ʿalā Muḥammad,
Ṣalla 'l-Lah ʿalāyhi wa sallam
Ṣalla 'l-Lah ʿalā Muḥammad,
Ṣalla 'l-Lah ʿalāyhi wa sallam

Allāhumma ṣalli ʿalā Muḥammadin wa-ʿalā
Sadātina 'alihi wa-ṣaḥbihi 'ahlit-tuqa
Allāhumma ṣalli ʿalā Muḥammadin wa-ʿalā
Sadātina 'alihi wa-ṣaḥbihi 'ahlil-wafa

Oh humans know we need Muhammad
Even today we need Muhammad
We go astray without Muhammad
We go astray, we go astray

Ṣalla 'l-Lah ʿalā Muḥammad,
Ṣalla 'l-Lah ʿalāyhi wa sallam
Ṣalla 'l-Lah ʿalā Muḥammad,
Ṣalla 'l-Lah ʿalāyhi wa sallam

Aḥmad Ya Ḥabibi (My Beloved)

Aḥmad ya ḥabibi salam 'alāyk
Aḥmad ya ḥabibi salam 'alāyk

You were sent as mercy,
mercy to all the worlds.
From the lord of mercy,
a gift to all the worlds.
Like the full moon you shine
in the darkness of the night.
This world could not exist,
if it wasn't for your light

Aḥmad ya ḥabibi salam 'alāyk
Aḥmad ya ḥabibi salam 'alāyk

Have you not heard Our Lord
telling His beloved Muhammad:
"they must first come to you
if they want me to forgive them"?
Have you not heard Our Lord
telling him to say:
"if what you seek is Allah's love,
you must first follow me"?

Aḥmad ya ḥabibi salam 'alāyk
Aḥmad ya ḥabibi salam 'alāyk

Like a mother loves her child,
you love humanity.
And that which you most desire
is for us to be happy.
We will suffer endlessly,
if with us you don't stand.
We'll be lost forever,
if you don't hold our hand

Aḥmad ya ḥabibi salam ʻalāyk
Aḥmad ya ḥabibi salam ʻalāyk

And you will intercede,
when no one else dares.
And you will succeed,
where all the others failed.
Raise your head My Beloved,
ask Me and you'll be given.
My Nation is what you'll ask,
send them My lord to heavens.

Aḥmad ya ḥabibi salam ʻalāyk
Aḥmad ya ḥabibi salam ʻalāyk

Yā Aba Zahra

يا أبا الزّهرا لله نظرَة   لا تخيبنا يا سيدي

نحن في بابك يا سيدي، نحن أحبابك

Yā Aba Zahra lillahi Nadhra La tukhayyibna Ya sidi
Naḥnu fi babak ya sidi, Naḥnu Aḥbabak
Oh Aba Zahra grant us a gaze for Allah's sake
do not disappoint us my master
We are at your door, we are those who love you

Oh beloved one,
your poor servant
stands at your door,
open for him.
His broken heart,
brought him this far.
Grant him your gaze,
and heal the scars

Yā Aba Zahra lillahi Nadhra La tukhayyibna yā sidi
Naḥnu fi babak ya sidi, Naḥnu aḥbabak

Your poor servant,
He's full of sins.
He carries with him
heavy burdens.
He asks forgiveness
In your presence.
Please ask for him
to be forgiven

Yā Aba Zahra lillahi Nadhra La tukhayyibna yā sidi
Naḥnu fi babak ya sidi, Naḥnu aḥbabak

Other than your door,
There are no doors.
In this ocean,
you're the only shore.
Mercy to all,
now and before
If you seek forgiveness,
then look no more

Yā Aba Zahra lillahi Nadhra La tukhayyibna yā sidi
Naḥnu fi babak ya sidi, Naḥnu aḥbabak

No where else to hide
No where to else to run
Abu Zahra
is the only one
Oh weak slaves,
run to his cave
if you love Muhammad,
you will be saved

Yā Aba Zahra lillahi Nadhra La tukhayyibna yā sidi
Naḥnu fi babak ya sidi, Naḥnu aḥbabak

Mercy Ocean

Come to mercy,
mercy Ocean.
Ocean of All the worlds,
mercy to All the worlds (2)

Muḥammad ṣall-Allāhu 'alayh
Muḥammad ṣall-Allāhu 'alayh
Muḥammad ṣall-Allāhu 'alayhi wa sallam

Come to forgiveness,
to the door of forgiveness.
Bring all your burdens here
and watch them disappear (2)

Muḥammad ṣall-Allāhu 'alayh
Muḥammad ṣall-Allāhu 'alayh
Muḥammad ṣall-Allāhu 'alayhi wa sallam

Come to goodness,
to the guide to goodness,
to the spring of beauty
to the spring of bliss (2)

Muḥammad ṣall-Allāhu 'alayh
Muḥammad ṣall-Allāhu 'alayh
Muḥammad ṣall-Allāhu 'alayhi wa sallam

Come to Love,
Sweetest love.
One drop is enough
to melt the world away (2)

Muḥammad ṣall-Allāhu 'alayh
Muḥammad ṣall-Allāhu 'alayh
Muḥammad ṣall-Allāhu 'alayhi wa sallam

Dedication

I humbly dedicate this mawlid book to the memory of Mawlana Shaykh Nazim Al-Haqqani (q). This book became a reality because of him. It was shaykh Nazim who encouraged me to write in praise of Sayyidna Muhammad. If it wasn't for Shaykh Nazim, I would have never understood the real meaning of love for Allah and His Prophet.

The sinful servant in need of Allah's mercy,
Ali Elsayed

Important Information

You can listen to and download the audio tracks to the Nasheeds in this book at:
https://www.alielsayed.com/mawlid
Website: : https://www.alielsayed.com
Email contact: alielsayednasheed@gmail.com
Facebook: https://www.facebook.com/shaykhalielsayed/
Youtube channel:
https://www.youtube.com/channel/UCfklZUEt-0npSwKd0xOfFmQ

If you appreciate this book, please leave a positive review on Amazon.

9 781732 160019

Printed by Libri Plureos GmbH in Hamburg,
Germany